GREAT MINDS OF SCIENCE

Robert Boyle
Pioneer of Experimental Chemistry

Mary Gow

Enslow Publishers, Inc.

40 Industrial Road   PO Box 38
Box 398   Aldershot
Berkeley Heights, NJ 07922   Hants GU12 6BP
USA   UK

Library of Congress Cataloging-in-Publication Data

Gow, Mary.
  Robert Boyle : pioneer of experimental chemistry / Mary Gow.
    p. cm. — (Great minds of science)
  Includes bibliographical references and index.
  ISBN 0-7660-2501-2
  1. Boyle, Robert, 1627–1691—Juvenile literature. 2. Scientists—Great Britain—Biography. 3. Boyle's law—Juvenile literature. I. Title. II. Series.
  Q143.B77G69 2005
  530'.092—dc22

                                                    2004009194

Printed in the United States of America

10 9 8 7 6 5 4 3 2 1

To Our Readers: We have done our best to make sure all Internet Addresses in this book were active and appropriate when we went to press. However, the author and the publisher have no control over and assume no liability for the material available on those Internet sites or on other Web sites they may link to. Any comments or suggestions can be sent by e-mail to comments@enslow.com or to the address on the back cover.

Illustration Credits: Chris Hughs from Hutchins' History of Dorset, p. 26; Courtesy of Lizzy Hewitt, pp. 32, 35, 37, 80, 94; Enslow Publishers, Inc., p. 59; Library of Congress, pp. 43, 70, 73; Lismore Castle, County Waterford (Eleanor and Clyde Moore, © 2004 <www.photosbyeleanor>), p. 16; Museum of the History of Science, Oxford, p. 9; Natick Historical Society, p. 85; National Library of Medicine, p. 75; National Oceanic and Atmospheric Administration (NOAA), pp. 50, 53, 63, 65, 82, 102; Wheeler Collection, Rare Books Division, The New York Public Library, Astor, Lenox and Tilden Foundations, p. 46.

Cover Illustration: Wheeler Collection, Rare Books Division, The New York Public Library, Astor, Lenox and Tilden Foundations (background); Courtesy of the Chemical Heritage Foundation Image Archives (inset).

Contents

"Which Seems to Prove . . ."

A GROUP OF MEN STOOD IN A laboratory in Oxford, England. Most knew each other, but a few curious strangers had stopped in, too. Everyone's attention was on a large, clear glass globe sitting on top of a thick tube. A tall, slender young man directed the experiment.

As the men observed, a thin string was tied to a ticking watch. The watch was lowered into the globe. The opening in the globe that the watch passed through was then sealed with a stopper. Wet plaster was packed around the stopper to make the globe airtight. Through the glass the group could see the dangling watch. It was out of its case, and they could see the watch's balance moving back and forth. They could hear the watch ticking. The slender man and a few of his guests pressed their ears to the glass to hear the sound even louder.

One man began pumping a handle beneath the globe. He was pumping air out of it. As the men watched and listened, "the sound grew fainter and fainter."[1] Finally, no one in the room "could, by applying our ears to the very sides, hear any noise from within," wrote their host. Looking at the watch, though, they "could easily perceive, that by the moving of the hand, which marked the second minutes. . . ," that it still ran.[2]

After a short time air was allowed back into the globe. The group could hear the ticking again.

The experiment was repeated, with the same results. "Which seems to prove," wrote Robert Boyle, the tall young scientist who had set up this demonstration, "that whether or [not] air be the only, it is at least the principal, medium of sounds."[3]

This experiment was conducted in Oxford, England, in the 1650s. Boyle's observation about sound explains why there is no sound when a meteor crashes into the moon or a spacewalking astronaut adjusts the energy panels on the International Space Station. Without air or another medium to conduct sound, there is silence.

The ticking watch experiment was listed as Experiment XXVII in Robert Boyle's first scientific book, *New Experiments Physico-Mechanical Touching the Spring of the Air*. Besides showing that air carries sound, Boyle's experiments revealed many other things about air. Some demonstrated that air had weight. Others showed that air could be compressed—squeezed into a smaller space. Some of these experiments showed that air is necessary for a candle to burn, a bee to fly, and a bird to breathe.

The Spring of the Air was a spectacular example of the new philosophy of studying nature through experiments. This approach to science was still a new idea in the 1600s. The book was also an outstanding example of Boyle's practice of sharing experimental knowledge. He believed in describing and publishing his experiments so others could learn from them. *The Spring of the Air* rapidly made Boyle famous. The book was the first of Boyle's valuable contributions to the development of science.

Born in his father's castle in Ireland in 1627, Robert Boyle was wealthy and aristocratic. He grew up to be a religious, charitable, and generous man. As an adult he discovered his passion for science—especially chemistry, the science of substances. Despite fragile health and poor eyesight, Boyle spent decades conducting scientific experiments and breaking new ground in scientific thought.

Boyle lived during a time of great change. The known world was expanding. England and other European countries were starting colonies in America. In 1627, the year Boyle was born, the settlement of English Pilgrims in Plymouth, Massachusetts, was just seven years old. Science was changing in the seventeenth century, too. New equipment and fresh ideas were helping

ROBERTVS BOYLE NOBILIS ANGLVS MD

A portrait of Robert Boyle with his air pump in the background.

people see the world in different ways. More and more Europeans were beginning to believe that the Sun, rather than Earth, stood in the middle of our planetary system.

Robert Boyle's work changed the way people thought about, and practiced, chemistry. He challenged the accepted ideas about chemistry. His experiments revealed worthwhile information about the characteristics of many substances. His observations of the relationship between the volume of an amount of air and the pressure exerted on it became known as Boyle's law. Boyle wrote and published extensively. His scientific works included books about the properties of air, colors, phosphorus, gold, and more. Boyle was a founder of the Royal Society, an organization that for more than three centuries has promoted excellence in the study of science.

Robert Boyle could have chosen a life of nobility, managing his estates and wealth. Instead, he pursued his fascination with chemistry. Along the way, he made discoveries and helped establish the experimental method in science.

One Who Loves Virtue

"MY WIFE, GOD EVER BE PRAISED, WAS about three of the clock in the afternoon of this day. . . safely delivered of her seventh son at Lismore," wrote the Earl of Cork in his diary on January 25, 1627. "God bless him," the earl continued, "for his name is Robert Boyle."[1]

This baby, like his fourteen brothers and sisters, was born to wealth and privilege. Lismore Castle, where Robert entered the world, was one of the grandest homes in Ireland. The stately stone manor house, with its turrets, defensive wall, and towered entry gate, looked down on the river Blackwater. Lismore Castle was home to the Great Earl of Cork, Sir Richard Boyle, the wealthiest man in all of England and Ireland.[2] When Robert was born, the earl's vast estates stretched almost all the way across southern Ireland.[3]

Although Richard Boyle lived in Ireland, the earl was English through and through. He was born in England and had gone to Ireland, when he was twenty-one years old. In Ireland, he made his fortune. Richard Boyle was a loyal subject of the King of England. He belonged to the Church of England, which was a Protestant religion, rather than the Roman Catholic Church, which was the faith of most of the Irish.

Richard Boyle married the beautiful Catherine Fenton in 1603. She was the daughter of a wealthy nobleman. On their wedding day, Richard was made a knight. Over the years he would be given many titles. He became Earl of Cork, Viscount Dungarvan, Baron of Youghal, and, for a time, Lord High Treasurer of Ireland. Richard and Catherine had fifteen children—twelve of them lived to be adults. Robert was the fourteenth child and youngest son.

"To be such parents' son and not their eldest, was a Happiness that [I] would mention with great expressions of gratitude,"[4] Robert Boyle wrote. He could not, he claimed, have chosen a situation more suited to his "inclinations and his designs." He was born, he wrote, "in a condition that was neither high enough to prove a temptation to laziness, nor low enough to discourage him from aspiring."[5]

The Boyles' extraordinary wealth gave Robert freedom from what he called "the inconveniences of a meane descent."[6] He would never, in his entire life, need to work for his living. He could follow his interests without worrying about cost. As a scientist, his wealth allowed him to equip laboratories and hire assistants for his research. He gave generously to people and causes he supported, and he became known for his great charity.

Robert Boyle considered himself lucky that he was not his parents' eldest son. "Being born heir to a great family is but a glittering kind of slavery," he wrote.[7] In England in the seventeenth century, eldest sons of noblemen inherited their father's titles and most of their lands. Boyle feared that eldest sons were so tied to their family responsibilities that they could not pursue their own interests.

We know much about Robert Boyle's childhood because he wrote his autobiography when he was in his early twenties. He called his manuscript "An Account of Philaretus During His Minority." In his writing, Robert Boyle called himself Philaretus. Philaretus is derived from ancient Greek and roughly translates to "one who loves virtue." Virtue means moral excellence—behaving in an honorable and good way.

Although Robert Boyle was born in Lismore Castle, he did not spend his early childhood in luxury. The earl "had a perfect aversion. . . to those who breed their children so nicely and tenderly that a hot sun or a good shower of rain as much endangers them as if they were made of butter or sugar," wrote Robert.[8] To toughen up baby Robert, the earl sent him to live with a "country nurse." Under her care he was fed a "coarse but cleanly diet" and exposed "to the usual passions of the air."[9] This upbringing was meant to make the boy heartier and healthier—whether it did is unclear. Robert Boyle had fragile health all his adult life. He often suffered from fevers and was easily chilled. As an adult, he was plagued by pain, which he believed was caused by kidney stones. However, in seventeenth-century England many children died of diseases that are prevented or easily cured today, so the country upbringing may have helped him survive.

Childhood outside the castle influenced the little boy. He later felt that he appreciated his privileges more because he had lived without them. "Hardships were made easy," he recalled, ". . . and the delights of conveniences and ease were endeared to him by their rarity."[10]

Before Robert returned to Lismore Castle, an event occurred that he considered the disaster of his young life. His mother died when he was three years old. Because of his country-nurse upbringing, Robert never knew her. Robert considered his other great misfortune to be his stutter. He believed that he stammered when he

Lismore Castle, the magnificent home where Robert Boyle was born. The castle was extensively remodeled in the early 1800s, so its appearance today is different than it was in Boyle's time.

spoke because he had made fun of the speech of a stuttering child. He thought his own stutter was God's punishment for his bad behavior. While Robert was growing up, his tutors gave him voice exercises to control his speech. One of his friends wrote that as an adult, Boyle "did sometimes a little hesitate rather than stammer."[11]

Robert rejoined his family after his mother's death. A few of his siblings were now adults.

The earl was managing his estates and serving as treasurer of Ireland. He was also arranging marriages for his older children. Marriages between wealthy nobles helped secure families' fortunes. Every one of Richard Boyle's children who married, married nobility.

From an early age Robert was noted for his honesty. His beloved older sister Katherine had a favorite story about her little brother's truthfulness. A particular plum tree of the Boyles' was bearing fruit. Katherine, twelve years older than Robert, decided that the plums should be saved for their sister-in-law Lady Dungarvan. Lady Dungarvan was married to Robert's oldest brother, and she was expecting a baby.

Robert, still a little boy, accidentally wandered into the garden. Although he knew that the plums were forbidden, he helped himself to them. Katherine caught him. She scolded him for eating "half a dozen" plums. "Nay truly, sister," he replied, "I have eaten half a score."[12] A score is twenty. Robert felt that telling a lie about the number of plums was worse than breaking the rule.

Robert's education began at Lismore. He was tutored at home, learning to write and speak French and Latin. Robert showed "a more than usual inclination" to study.[13] After a few years of homeschooling, the earl sent Robert and his brother Francis to Eton College. Eton is in England, near London. The earl knew the headmaster there. Robert and Francis were accompanied by a private tutor, who rented their rooms, purchased their clothes, and handled many of the details of their lives for them. Their tutor, Mr. Carew, regularly reported to the earl. Robert "prefers learning above all other virtues or pleasures," Carew wrote.[14]

During the boys' second year at Eton the headmaster changed. The earl, in the meantime, had purchased land and a manor house in Stalbridge, England. Robert and Francis visited their father there. Shortly after their visit the earl withdrew them from school. Robert's two years at Eton were the only formal education he would ever have.

Robert Boyle was eleven years old when he and Francis moved to Stalbridge. The earl was seventy. "The good old earl," Robert wrote about his father, "welcomed him very kindly."[15] Richard Boyle's fondness for his youngest son was apparent. The earl considered Robert "very much his favorite."[16]

At Stalbridge, Robert and Francis were tutored again. Then their education was passed to Isaac Marcombes. Marcombes had tutored their older brothers. He would take the boys on a grand tour of Europe. Accompanied by servants, they would study and live on the continent.

At the same time, the earl had arranged a prestigious marriage for Francis. On October 24, 1639, in London, a grand wedding celebrated the marriage of Francis and his bride, Elizabeth Killigrew. King Charles I attended the festivities. Four days later, twelve-year-old Robert and sixteen-year-old Francis left London with Marcombes to continue their education in Europe. Elizabeth was left behind to wait for her husband's return.

Robert Boyle's time in Europe had a profound influence on him. With Marcombes, he and Francis traveled in France and Italy. They stayed more than twenty months in Geneva at their tutor's home. The boys studied Latin, rhetoric, and history. Robert spoke French almost all the time. He became so fluent that people often thought he was a Frenchman. Every day the boys read from the Bible. Robert also studied mathematics.

One summer night in Geneva when Robert was thirteen years old, a violent thunderstorm struck. Robert "was suddenly waked in a fright with such loud claps of thunder. . . and every clap was both preceded and attended with flashes of lightning so numerous and so dazzling that [I] began to imagine them the sallies of fire that must consume the world."[17] The violence of the storm convinced Robert "of the day of Judgment's being at hand."[18]

Robert was raised in the religion of the Church of England. He had studied the Bible. During the raging storm Robert feared the world was ending. He decided that he was unprepared for God's judgment, as he believed it to be. That notion made him "resolve and vow, that . . . all further additions to his life should be more religiously and carefully employed."[19]

The storm eventually passed. The next morning dawned calm and cloudless. Robert thought about the vow he had made the night before. He reconfirmed his decision to lead his life in a more religious way. It was a vow that influenced the rest of his years. From that day on, his lifestyle, his philosophy, and much of his writing were closely tied to his religious faith.

After nearly two years in Geneva, Marcombes took Robert and Francis on a tour of Italy. They had convinced their father to allow, and pay, for the trip. The boys were elegantly outfitted with new wardrobes. In their travels they climbed mountains, visited Venice, and admired antiquities and architecture.

One of their stops, in 1642, was the city of Florence. Galileo Galilei, the astronomer and mathematician, was living just outside of Florence. Galileo had used a telescope to study the heavens. Through it he saw craters on the moon, the phases of Venus, Jupiter's moons, and more. Galileo wrote a book called *Starry Messenger* about some of his earliest observations. His later book *Dialogue Concerning the Two Chief Systems of the World—Ptolemaic and Copernican* discussed whether Earth or the Sun is at the center of our system. Galileo believed that Earth and the other planets revolved around the Sun. Galileo also did experiments and wrote about motion and acceleration.

In Florence, young Robert Boyle read Galileo's books. He was intrigued by what he called the "paradoxes of the great star-gazer."[20] Reading Galileo's works may have been the beginning of Robert Boyle's fascination with science. Galileo, age seventy-eight, died while Robert was still in Florence. The two never met.

From Florence, Robert, Francis, and Marcombes continued their travels in Italy, then sailed to France. Arriving in Marseille, they expected money from the earl to pay for their return home. Alarming news found them instead.

Violent rebellions had erupted in Ireland.

The Irish were rising up against the rule of King Charles I and his noblemen, like Richard Boyle. The earl and his older sons had returned to Ireland. They had raised armies and were fighting to defend their castles and land.[21] The earl sent money for the boys to come to Ireland. When his letter found them, the money was gone. A dishonest agent in London was suspected of taking it.

With their remaining funds, Francis left immediately for Ireland. Robert had fallen ill. He was too weak to travel and knew that he was not old enough to fight. Marcombes took him back to Geneva. Robert continued his studies there for almost two more years.

"Transported and Bewitched"

ROBERT BOYLE RETURNED TO ENGLAND in 1644. He was seventeen years old and an orphan. He had been away for almost five years. During his absence his father, the Earl of Cork, had died. The earl left the estate at Stalbridge and a share of his other wealth to Robert. Besides a changed family, Robert Boyle returned to a changed country. England was in the midst of a civil war.

In London, Robert looked up his favorite sister, Katherine, Lady Ranelagh. He appeared at her mansion still dressed in his French clothing—nobody recognized him. When he spoke, Katherine "look'd upon him with surprise." Then, he recalled, "she cried out, 'Oh! 'Tis my brother,' with the joy and tenderness of a most affectionate sister."[1] Katherine insisted he stay with her, and he did for several months. The fondness between Robert and Katherine lasted all their lives.

Lady Ranelagh was bright and charming. A friend wrote that Katherine "was one of the most beautiful as well as the most talented of her time."[2] Her memory was extraordinary; she could listen to a church sermon, then go home and write it down exactly as it was spoken. Her marriage, though, was miserable. The same friend wrote that Katherine's husband, Lord Ranelagh, was "the foulest churl in Christiandom."[3] Fortunately for Katherine, Lord Ranelagh usually stayed in Ireland. He let her live in London.

In London, Katherine had a vast circle of friends. Some of her close friends and her in-laws were in Parliament. Parliament is the legislative body of Great Britain—the branch of the government that makes laws. Struggles

The Stalbridge manor house that Robert Boyle inherited from his father.

between King Charles I and the Parliament were at the heart of England's civil war. The king raised armies that were loyal to him. The Parliamentarians raised their own armies. Battles were being fought, and the country was divided. Religious divisions in England were also part of this clash. Over twenty thousand Puritans left England and moved to North America during Charles I's rule.[4]

Among Katherine's friends were thinkers,

who were interested in science, like Samuel Hartlib. Hartlib was enthusiastic about education and about using science in farming. He was also a communicator of scientific ideas and exchanged letters with people in England and around Europe. When he received interesting news, which was often, he sent it on to others. Hartlib's correspondence served as a kind of scientific newsletter. Through Hartlib, Boyle met other scientists and natural philosophers of his day.

The word *scientist* was not actually used until 1840. In Boyle's time, scientific thinkers were called natural philosophers. Natural philosophy was the study of nature and the physical world and universe.

Robert Boyle finally settled in at Stalbridge nearly two years after returning to England. The manor house was not very welcoming. It bustled with family, servants, and gardeners when Boyle had visited his father there.[5] Since the earl's death, the estate had been neglected.

At Stalbridge, Robert Boyle's scientific life began. In the gentle countryside of southwest

England, he discovered his passion for experimenting.

We do not know what led Robert Boyle to chemistry. It was possibly a combination of his own reading and ideas he was learning from his new science-minded friends. However, it appears that he planned to at least dabble in chemistry when he moved to Stalbridge. In outfitting the manor house, he had ordered equipment for a laboratory—an earthen furnace, special glass containers, and more. The furnace was important because he would use it to heat and combine substances.

Chemistry is the science of substances. Chemists study the composition and properties of substances—what they are made of and their characteristics. Chemists also study change—how substances behave under different conditions.

Robert wanted to start experimenting. He waited impatiently for his equipment. The furnace was coming from a thousand miles away. It was so slow arriving that he complained to Katherine that he thought its carriage must be pulled by snails.[6] When the furnace finally arrived in Stalbridge, it was broken, "brought to my hands crumbled," he wrote to her. "I have been so unlucky in my first attempts in chemistry."[7] Even without the furnace, he did "such experiments as the unfurnishedness of the place and the present distraction of my mind will permit me."[8]

When at last a working furnace arrived, it changed Boyle's life. "Vulcan has so transported and bewitched me," he wrote to Katherine, "that as the delights I taste in it make me fancy my laboratory a kind of Elysium."[9] Vulcan was the name for the Roman god of metalworking. Boyle was referring to the furnace's fire as Vulcan. Elysium was also from Roman mythology—a place of boundless joy and bliss.

What were the experiments that transported Boyle to such a state of bliss? A list that he wrote at Stalbridge indicates that some involved salts, others had to do with medicines, and that he also did some distillation.[10] Distillation is a process of heating and then cooling a substance to get a purer version of it. Experiments with gold were also among Boyle's chemical explorations at Stalbridge.[11]

Some of Robert Boyle's experiments at Stalbridge and later in his life involved alchemy. Today, alchemy is often considered a false science practiced by mystics who were trying to make gold from worthless metals. That view is only partly accurate. In Boyle's time chemistry and alchemy were very close. Both were descended from the teaching of ancient Greek philosophers, including Aristotle. Aristotle believed in reason and logic. He had suggested that all substances were made of four different elements—earth, water, air, and fire. These were the elements supposedly present in all things, just in different amounts. Following this idea, it seemed reasonable that by manipulating those four elements you could change one substance to another. This was called transmutation.

Early alchemy was influenced by Egyptian craftsmen. Some skilled craftsmen knew recipes to combine metals and create the appearance of gold. Some people probably believed that the craftsmen really changed those other metals to gold. Over the centuries many alchemists tried to make gold. Gold was valuable, and it was also thought to have healing powers. Alchemy became secretive. Alchemists usually did not write down or share their recipes.

Boyle did not accept Aristotle's idea of four elements, but he did believe it could be possible to change one substance to another. He was not interested in making gold to become rich. However, he was intrigued with transmutation. In one of his Stalbridge experiments, Boyle combined mercury and gold. Together, the two substances became hot in his hand. This observation, he thought, might be a step toward transmutation. It was memorable enough to him that he wrote about it nearly twenty-five years later.

When Boyle was not performing experiments, he often took long walks. He managed the estate, read persistently, and wrote. Some of his writings were letters to friends, like Hartlib. He also wrote about religious subjects. At Stalbridge, he wrote essays about how to live a moral life. Many of these were later published.

The view down High Street in Oxford. Boyle lived in rented rooms on High Street between 1655 and 1668.

A Free Discourse against Swearing explained his view of why swearing was sinful. Another was titled *Some Motives and Incentives to the Love of God*. He wrote a novel called *The Martyrdom of Theodora and Didymus*. It was a romance, but had a religious theme.

In 1649 King Charles I was executed for treason. There is no record of Robert Boyle's thoughts about the execution.

Stalbridge remained Boyle's home for a few more years. He traveled occasionally to London and also went to Ireland to deal with the family's estates there. In Ireland, he met William Petty, a physician and surgeon. Boyle and Petty had exchanged letters for years. In Ireland, Petty taught Boyle about anatomy and blood circulation. They dissected animals together.[12]

During the trip to Ireland, perhaps with Petty's encouragement, Boyle was considering a change. His enthusiasm for experimenting had blossomed. He was becoming respected by scientists, but it was hard for his scientific interests to grow working alone at Stalbridge.

Boyle had two options. He could go to

London and meet scientists there. However, the city was still in turmoil due to the civil war. His other choice was Oxford. The city of Oxford, about fifty miles from London, is home to the oldest English-speaking university in the world. Colleges in Oxford have been educating students since the early 1200s. By Boyle's time there were fifteen colleges there. Oxford was then, and is now, a lively center of learning.

"I should exceedingly rejoice in your being stayed in England this winter," John Wilkins, the head of Wadham College, wrote to Boyle. Wilkins looked forward to "the advantage of your conversation at Oxford." In Oxford, explained Wilkins, Boyle would "meet with diverse persons who will truly love and honour you."[13]

Wilkins was highly regarded for his intelligence and, as one friend wrote, "his universal insight into all parts of learning."[14] As head of Wadham College, Wilkins brought intellectual excitement to Oxford. He arranged weekly meetings for interested scholars to

The square plaque on this wall marks the site of Robert Boyle's home in Oxford, where he once lived in rooms that he rented on High Street.

exchange ideas about the new experimental philosophy.[15]

Boyle did not go to Oxford as either a student or a professor. He moved to Oxford as a wealthy gentleman who had turned to science.[16]

Wilkins invited Boyle to live at Wadham College, but he rented rooms on High Street instead. The house was between University College and the Three Tuns Tavern.[17] Later, Boyle would also rent a retreat at Stanton St. John's, four miles away. He rented the second home because he occasionally needed to escape the constant flow of visitors to his rooms.

Oxford was the perfect place for Boyle. Some of the seventeenth century's most brilliant English thinkers were there. Besides Wilkins, the group included the chemist Thomas Willis, mathematician Seth Ward, and Richard Lower, who did early research in blood transfusions. Christopher Wren was in his early twenties when Boyle arrived. Wren, like Boyle, would soon be regarded as one of the wonders of the age.[18] Wren was a mathematician, astronomer, architect, and scientist.

The plaque at the site of Boyle's rooms on High Street in Oxford. The plaque is mounted on the wall of University College.

Beyond their specific interests, the group that met weekly with Wilkins shared a view of natural philosophy. They believed that observation and reason were the keys to truth.[19]

In the company of brilliant thinkers and new ideas, Boyle's first years in Oxford were like an intense apprenticeship. Up to this point, his knowledge about science came from his independent work—his extensive reading, his own experiments, and his correspondence with other intellectuals, or thinkers. At Oxford, he met with great men. He hired a tutor to help him learn geometry and chemistry. His tutor also helped him learn about the new natural philosophy and the ideas of René Descartes.[20]

The ideas of René Descartes and Francis Bacon influenced many of the thinkers who were living in Oxford. Descartes was a French philosopher who believed that the physical universe was a complex system governed by mathematical laws. He believed that laws of motion and laws of geometry could explain almost everything about the material world. The writings of Francis Bacon also influenced the scientific ideas of many seventeenth-century thinkers. Bacon was among the first philosophers to argue that science should be based on experimental evidence, not just old ideas.

4

The Spring of the Air

IN OXFORD, ROBERT BOYLE SET UP A laboratory in which to do his experiments. He also had the spectacular good fortune to have a brilliant young man as his assistant. Robert Hooke was in his early twenties when he began working with Boyle. Hooke was studying at Oxford but was already included in the circle of scholars who met weekly to discuss science. Part of Hooke's genius was that he had an extraordinary talent for making machines. It has been said that every important scientific instrument of the time was improved by Robert Hooke.[1] Telescopes, microscopes, pocket watches, barometers, and thermometers were all made better by Hooke. Hooke would also make amazing discoveries of his own.

Chemistry was Boyle's greatest scientific interest, but he had almost unlimited curiosity. In Oxford, he read about the experiments of Otto von Guericke and Evangelista Torricelli. These demonstrations led Boyle to temporarily quit chemistry for pneumatics—the study of the properties of air and other gases.

Many ideas about air in Boyle's time came from ancient Greek ideas about matter. Aristotle considered air one of the four basic elements, along with water, earth, and fire. In this scheme, air was thought to be weightless. Aristotle's view was that a vacuum was a contradiction in logic. A vacuum is a space with nothing in it. Over the centuries, Aristotle's view was stretched to include the principle that "nature abhors a vacuum."[2] Many people thought that a vacuum could not exist in nature.

In the 1600s more and more people began to think that air had weight. Evangelista Torricelli in Italy and Otto von Guericke in Germany were two of these men. Boyle heard about, and was inspired by, their experiments.

Von Guericke, the mayor of a German town called Magdeburg, had made an air pump. His device was "a way of emptying glass vessels by sucking out the air at the mouth of the vessel, plunged under water," wrote Boyle.[3]

In 1657 von Guericke conducted an impressive demonstration that showed the force of air pressure. He had a special sphere made from copper. The sphere was actually two hemispheres that fit smoothly together, with no gaps. On one of the hemispheres was a valve with the air pump attached to it.

At the start of von Guericke's demonstration, the sphere was full of air. Unless they were held together, the two halves fell apart. Von Guericke wanted to show that if the air was pumped out of the sphere, then the air pressure outside of it would hold the halves together.

The two halves of the copper sphere were held in place. Then, air was pulled out of the sphere with the pump. After as much air as possible was removed, the halves of the sphere would not separate. In a dramatic display, von Guericke hitched teams of horses to the two sides of the sphere. Eight horses pulled to the left and eight horses pulled to the right. The hemispheres would not come apart until air was allowed back into them. With his sphere and horses, von Guericke had masterfully demonstrated the great force of air pressure.

To a very small degree, you see what von Guericke demonstrated every time you drink through a straw. When you suck on the straw, you are not actually pulling liquid up into it. Instead, with your mouth and lungs you are removing the air from the straw. The air above and around you is pressing on the liquid in the glass. The force of that pressure pushes the liquid up the straw and into your mouth.

Boyle was fascinated that an air pump could show the force of air. He wanted one, but he wanted one different from von Guericke's.[4] Boyle wanted his air pump attached to a glass vessel. He could set up experiments inside a glass container and observe them as air was pumped out or in.

The Magdeburg demonstration of von Guericke's spheres. Details of the brass hemispheres are shown above the scene. After air was pumped out of the sphere, two teams of eight horses each were unable to pull the hemispheres apart.

Boyle first hired an instrument maker in London to make his air pump. The instrument he produced was far too clumsy. Then, Boyle wisely turned to his capable assistant, Robert Hooke.

Hooke's air pump was a revolutionary piece of equipment. It changed science. As the invention of the telescope made it possible to see objects far from earth that were unseen before, Hooke's air pump made it possible to see the effects of air as never before.

The air pump is generally seen as Boyle's invention, even though it was designed by Hooke. The thought is that Boyle decided what was needed, and Hooke figured out how to do it. When Boyle realized the spectacular success of his experiments, in his books he mentioned Hooke's role in designing the pump.

Hooke also probably helped Boyle with the experiments with the pump. Boyle mentions that his eyes were bothering him a great deal during this time. Because of his vision, he often dictated the descriptions and results of his experiments and they were recorded by an assistant.

Boyle's air pump was not a complicated machine. Water pumps had existed for centuries. Hooke's design, like von Guericke's, drew on that knowledge. The pump was a piston that fit snugly inside a hollow cylinder. The piston was raised and lowered by moving the pump handle. The pump was a little like a bicycle pump in reverse.

What was so valuable about Boyle's pump was that it attached to a strong glass sphere. His pump could empty the glass container of almost all air. He could observe the effects of air on experiments inside the container. Boyle had a marvelous mind for experimenting. Many of Boyle's experiments were simple, but they amazed observers because they had never been seen before.

"We took then a lamb's bladder large, well dried, and very limber, and leaving in it about half as much air as it could contain, we caused the neck of it to be strongly tied, so that none of the included air, though by pressure, could get

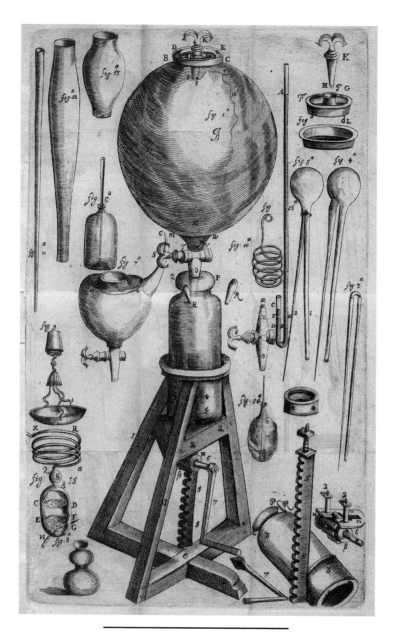

Robert Boyle's air pump, made by Robert Hooke. Experiments were conducted in the glass globe. The ticking watch, lighted candles, insects, lamb's bladder and other subjects of his experiments could be lowered into the globe through the hole at its top. The pump was in the cylinder below the globe.

out," Boyle wrote, describing one experiment.[5] Today, this could be done with a sealed plastic sandwich bag, but plastic bags were not available to Boyle. The half-filled, sealed lamb's bladder was placed in the glass container. As the air was pumped out of the container, "the imprisoned air began to swell in the bladder."[6] As more air was pumped out, it swelled more and more, until "the bladder appeared as full and stretched as if it had been blown up."[7] When air was released back into the glass container, the bladder drooped back to its flaccid form. What had Boyle observed? Describing the experiment, he said it was the "spring of the air." When there was less air in the glass container, there was less air pressure on the bladder. The air inside the bladder could—and did—expand. However, when air was allowed back in, the pressure on the bladder was increased and "the bladder was proportionally compressed."[8]

Boyle's other experiments with the air pump included the demonstration with the ticking watch. He did not understand how breathing worked, but he observed that birds in the sphere died without air. He did one experiment with a magnet and noted that there was no difference in its behavior if there was air or not. Several of his experiments showed that flames were extinguished when the air was removed.

The experiments Boyle considered most important were follow-up to the work of Evangelista Torricelli. Torricelli was a talented Italian mathematician. He worked as Galileo's secretary during the last months of the astronomer's life. (Had young Robert Boyle visited Galileo when he was in Florence, he probably would have met Torricelli.)

Galileo and Torricelli had discussed a phenomenon regarding water pumps. Suction water pumps only raise water about thirty-four feet. Galileo thought this might be related to the "force of a vacuum."[9]

Torricelli set up an experiment in 1643 to explore this idea. He could have done this experiment with water, but chose to use mercury because mercury is about fourteen times heavier than water. Mercury is a heavy metal that is liquid at room temperature. It is the silver liquid that you see in thermometers. Doing the experiment with water would require a tube thirty-five feet tall. With mercury Torricelli only needed a tube about three feet tall.

Torricelli's glass tube was sealed at one end. The tube was filled with mercury. When it was filled to the rim, an assistant put his finger over the open end and inverted the tube—turned it upside down. The open end, now at the bottom, was placed in an open bowl of mercury. When the assistant removed his finger, some of the mercury flowed out of the tube and into the bowl. Although the level of the mercury in the tube had dropped, there was still a column of mercury about thirty inches tall standing in the tube. When the experiment was repeated, the same amount of mercury stayed in the vertical tube.

Torricelli's experiment raised two questions. First, since the sealed tube had held only mercury, but now the level was lower, what was in the empty space? Second, why did the mercury in the tube repeatedly drop to about the same level?

The answer to the first question seems simple

EN VIRESCIT GALILÆVS ALTER
Anagr.
EVANGELISTA TORRICELLIVS
Sereniſſimi M. Ducis Hetruriæ
Mathem.ᵘˢ & Philos.ᵘˢ
Obijt Anno Dom. MDCXLVII. Aet. XL

Evangelista Torricelli's experiments showed that the weight of the atmosphere is measurable. By inverting a tube containing mercury over an open dish of mercury, he showed that atmospheric pressure supported a column of nearly 30 inches of mercury. His experiments also demonstrated that a vacuum could exist.

now, but was contrary to the accepted ideas of the time. What was in the empty portion of the tube? Nothing—but nothing was not an expected answer. Many people did not believe that a vacuum, a space with nothing in it, could exist. No other substance could have leaked into Torricelli's tube. With this experiment Torricelli was the first person to create a sustained vacuum.[10]

Why did the mercury in the tube drop to the same level over and over? It stopped there for the same reason that von Guericke's sphere could not be pulled apart. Atmospheric pressure was pushing down on the open bowl. Torricelli explained, "I claim that the force which keeps the mercury from falling is external and that the force comes from outside the tube. On the surface of the mercury which rests in the bowl rests the weight of a column of fifty miles of air."[11] Torricelli correctly believed that on earth's surface, we live at the bottom of a sea of air.

Torricelli's experiment, when repeated in different weather conditions, revealed that air pressure was not always the same. Sometimes air pressure supported a taller column of mercury and sometimes a shorter column. Again, Torricelli was right when he recognized that the atmosphere "is at some times heavier and denser and at other times lighter and thinner."[12] Air pressure changes with different weather. The instrument that Torricelli invented, the barometer, measures changing atmospheric pressure, and is a valuable tool used to predict weather. Torricelli died in 1647, shortly after making these discoveries.

Robert Boyle was eager to continue Torricelli's research. With his air pump he did several experiments based on Torricelli's work. In one experiment Boyle took a three-foot-long glass tube. He filled it with mercury and inverted it in a box of mercury. The box and tube were lowered into the glass sphere. The top of the sphere was sealed so air could not get in even though the tube stuck out the top. As they started pumping air out of the container, the level of mercury in the tube dropped. When they let air back in, the level rose. Boyle's air pump experiment confirmed Torricelli's work.

This engraving from a 1688 book by Joachim d'Alence illustrates the principle of the barometer. Both tubes are sealed at the top. The tube at the left is open at the bottom and is sitting in a bowl of mercury. The weight of the atmosphere pressing down on the mercury in the bowl is sufficient to support a column of nearly thirty inches of mercury.

In 1660 Boyle published his research with the air pump in his first scientific book. He called it *On the Spring and Weight of the Air*. The book was an instant success. With it Boyle became one of the best-known scientists of the day.[13]

Boyle's Law

ROBERT BOYLE UNDOUBTEDLY FELT HIS ears pop from time to time. He had certainly experienced it when he and his brother Francis had climbed mountains in Italy during their time with Marcombes. We know that Boyle was fascinated with the night sky even though his eyes often troubled him. With a telescope he saw and marveled at "numberless little stars" that could not be seen with the unassisted eye.[1] Boyle had diverse scientific interests. It seems fitting that the natural law he discovered helps explain phenomena from ear popping to the life cycle of stars.

The discovery of Boyle's law was a result of Boyle's book *The Spring of the Air*. The book brought Boyle far-reaching praise. His friend Hartlib sent copies of it to many intellectuals. One of them wrote back that Boyle "hath given us hope, that we shall shortly complete human sciences."[2] Throughout England and across Europe, scientists shared this enthusiasm.

One person who doubted Boyle's experiments was Franciscus Linus. Linus taught at the University of Liege. He believed in the Aristotelian scheme of four elements. Linus was willing to accept that air has some spring and weight, but he did not believe that its strength could be as great as Boyle claimed.

Boyle was a polite man and not prone to bitterness. He responded to Linus by demonstrating the properties of air more convincingly. He set up an experiment to show that air could support considerable weight. Hooke was Boyle's assistant at this time. Hooke probably had a great deal to do with this experiment.[3]

Boyle presented a report of this experiment

to the Royal Society in September 1661. A full description of the experiment and his response to Linus were included in a second edition of *The Spring of the Air*, published in 1662.

This experiment did not require the air pump. Boyle took a long glass tube, and had a glassworker bend it, so it was shaped like a tall J. The short end of the tube was sealed. The other end was open. The tube was so tall, Boyle wrote, "that we could not conveniently make use of it in a chamber." Instead, he explained, "we were fain to use it on a pair of stairs."[4] Like Torricelli, Boyle used mercury for the experiment because it is much heavier than water.

One person, probably Boyle, stood at the bottom of the tube to take measurements. Another person, probably Hooke, was at the top. First, a little mercury was poured into the tube to fill the curve at the bottom of the J. Filling this low spot trapped a pocket of air in the short leg of the J. Boyle wrote down the exact length of the tube that held trapped air and the length of tube that was filled with mercury. Their measurements were in eighths of inches.

Up the stairs, mercury was added, "by little and little," into the long end of the tube.[5] As mercury was added, the space occupied by the air grew smaller and smaller. Adding mercury to the tube increased the pressure on the little pocket of air. In other words, more mercury meant more weight pushing on the trapped air. Finally, Boyle observed, "the air was so compressed, as to be crowded into less than a quarter of the space that it possessed before."[6] As Hooke added mercury Boyle recorded the inches of air and inches of mercury in the tube.

The experiment was a success. It demonstrated what Boyle intended—that the pocket of air could hold up a considerable weight of mercury.

Something more was revealed by this experiment. When Boyle looked at the measurements of the air and mercury, he could see that there was a relationship between the volume of the air and the pressure on it.

That discovery is now called Boyle's law. Boyle's law is often stated, the volume of a gas varies inversely with the pressure on the gas.[7]

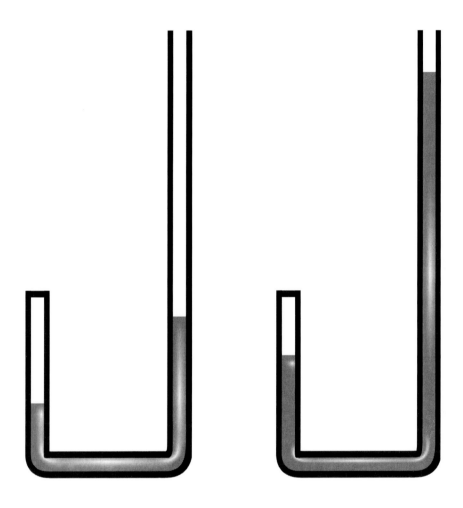

The experiment that Boyle conducted with the long J-shaped tube of mercury showed that air could be compressed. It also revealed that there was a relationship between the amount of pressure on the air and the volume of the air. As more mercury was added to the tube, the air was compressed into a smaller space. This relationship is known as Boyle's Law.

Another way of saying this is, as the pressure upon a gas goes up, the volume of the gas goes down in the same proportion.

Why is Boyle's law true? Gases are made of constantly moving particles. These particles are atoms and molecules. Atoms are the smallest amount of an element that can exist and still retain the element's characteristics. Molecules are the smallest amounts of a compound that can exist and still retain the compound's characteristics. Air is a mixture of several gases. Nitrogen, oxygen, hydrogen, and carbon dioxide are among the elements and compounds in air. Atoms and molecules in gases move around. There are spaces between them. If there is little pressure on the atoms and molecules, they move over greater spaces. If the pressure on a gas is increased, the atoms and molecules get crowded together and there is less space between them.

When you think about Boyle's law, remember that we live at the bottom of a sea of air. On the surface of earth, the air in our atmosphere is pressing against everything around us. At sea level, air pressure is an average of 14.7 pounds per square inch. (Remember that this changes slightly with the weather, as Evangelista Torricelli observed.) We are not aware of this pressure because it is pressing on all sides of us.

This pressure is not the same everywhere on our planet. Air pressure is lower at high elevations, like on mountaintops. At the top of Mount Everest, 29,028 feet high, the air pressure is about one-third of that at sea level. Under water, pressure is much higher than 14.7 pounds per square inch. Water is far heavier than air. A depth of only 33 feet of water exerts an additional 14.7 pounds of pressure.

Let us look at Boyle's law and how it would apply to a cubic foot of air at different places on earth. Imagine you are going on an adventure. You start your adventure at the beach. Because the beach is by the ocean, you are at sea level. Someone gives you a very flexible balloon with some air in it. At sea level, the volume of gas in your balloon is exactly one cubic foot. (A cubic foot is a space that if it had the shape of a cube, it would measure one foot long, one foot wide, and one foot deep.)

After you have had enough sun and sand, you leave the ocean to climb Mount Everest. You take your balloon full of air with you. As you climb Mount Everest you notice that from time to time your ears pop. At the top of the mountain, you look at your balloon. Atmospheric pressure on the top of Everest is about one-third of what it was at the beach. With less pressure on it, the air in your balloon has expanded to occupy three cubic feet. Your flexible balloon has stretched to accommodate this change. Your ears, however, have not stretched. You have several air spaces in your body. The Eustachian tubes in your ears are among them. When you climbed the mountain, the air inside your Eustachian tubes was expanding just like the air in your balloon. Every now and then your ears popped to release some of the extra volume of air. They may pop going back down as the air inside them is compressed again.

After your mountain-climbing expedition, you go back to the beach. Once again under 14.7 pounds per inch of air pressure, your balloon now holds one cubic foot of air.

Scuba divers need to be conscious of Boyle's law. Human lungs are similar to balloons. If a diver fills her lungs at the surface, then dives to a depth of thirty-three feet, the air in the lungs will only occupy half the space filled at the surface. If the diver then breathes from her air tanks, she can again fill her lungs to their capacity.

Next, you decide to scuba dive. In your scuba-diving lessons, your instructor teaches you about Boyle's law. He wants you to remember certain safety precautions. Once you have passed your scuba test, you take your balloon with you for a dive. Thirty-three feet below the surface, you look at your balloon. It is only half as big as it was at the surface. Remember that at thirty-three feet there is twice as much pressure on you and your balloon as there was at the surface.

When you begin to return to the surface, you remember what your instructor taught you about Boyle's law. As you go up, the air in your balloon is expanding. The air in your lungs is expanding, too. The balloon is more flexible than your lungs. You must remember to keep breathing in and out so that you do not trap air in your lungs. If you hold your breath as you ascend, the trapped air will expand and injure your lungs.

When Robert Boyle discovered this relationship between air and pressure, he did not express it as a universal law that applies to all gases. He was describing his observation of how air behaves. It turns out that his discovery applies to other gases, too.

After Boyle's discovery many more things were learned about gases. In 1787 French balloonist Professor Jacques Alexandre César Charles made observations on the relationship between the temperature and volume of gases.

Professor Jacques Charles, one of the first balloonists ever, is credited with discovering the gas law that describes the relationship between temperature and volume of gases. Charles's Law and Boyle's Law are combined in the Ideal Gas Law of Chemistry.

In simple terms, Charles's law says that if you heat a gas, its volume increases. Charles never actually wrote down this law, but it is named for him anyway.

Today, Charles's law and Boyle's law are often used together in the Ideal Gas Law of Chemistry. This law describes the relationship between pressure, volume, and temperature for an ideal gas. Although no gas is perfectly ideal, real gases act closely enough to the ideal that the law helps scientists study the behavior of gases in many ways. The Ideal Gas Law helps scientists study the life cycle of stars and the eruption of volcanoes. It helps engineers design refrigerators, air conditioners, and jet engines.

Boyle did not know that this relationship between a gas's volume and pressure would be named for him. Boyle believed that the world was complex but that it was created with certain mathematical and scientific rules. Boyle's law describes one of those rules.

The Sceptical Chymist

AS SUCCESSFUL AS BOYLE WAS WITH HIS experiments with air, chemistry drew him back. In 1661, during the same time that Boyle achieved fame from his air experiments, he published a book called *The Sceptical Chymist*. In this book he refuted the accepted seventeenth-century approach to chemistry. He showed that chemistry should be based on experiments. Today, *The Sceptical Chymist* is probably Boyle's most famous book. Part of its present fame, though, comes from a misunderstanding of one of his statements.

"Remember that it is a sceptic speaks to you,"

says the book's main character. He continues, "it is not so much my present task to make assertions as to raise doubts."[1] Raising doubts was what Boyle wanted to do. A *sceptic*—or *skeptic*—as it is spelled today—is a person who questions accepted ideas.

Most of *The Sceptical Chymist* is a discussion of the most widely accepted ideas about chemistry at the time. A group of friends have gathered in the garden at the home of Carneades, the skeptic. The men have different views of chemistry and substances.

One character, Themistius, believes in the approach to chemistry that was based on Aristotle's writings. This theory held that there were four elements—fire, air, earth, and water. These elements were believed to be in all things. What made substances different from each other was the amount of each element in a substance and how moisture and heat affected them.

Philoponus, a third character in Boyle's book, was a Paracelsian. He believed in the teaching of a man named Paracelsus, who lived in the 1500s. Much of Paracelsian chemistry dealt with medicines. This chemistry was based on the idea that all bodies were composed of three "principles." These three principles were called salt, sulfur, and mercury.

Eleutherius, another member of the group, serves as a kind of judge in the discussion. A fifth character is the narrator, who reports the conversation. (Although the narrator is not named, it may be Boyle, himself.[2])

The Sceptical Chymist is difficult to read and understand. The terms of seventeenth-century chemistry are unfamiliar to most modern readers. The book does not have much of a plot. Two of the main characters, Themistius and Philoponus, are not present through most of the story. Their ideas about chemistry are discussed in their absence. Some scholars believe that Boyle combined two separate manuscripts in *The Sceptical Chymist* and that this partly explains why it is confusing. In the book's introduction Boyle comments that the work is "maim'd and imperfect."[3]

In spite of its problems, *The Sceptical Chymist* became an important work in the history of

THE
Sceptical Chymist:
OR
CHYMICO-PHYSICAL
Doubts & Paradoxes;
Touching the
EXPERIMENTS
WHEREBY
VULGAR SPAGIRISTS
Are wont to Endeavour to Evince their
SALT, SULPHUR
AND
MERCURY,
TO BE

The True Principles of Things.
To which in this Edition are subjoyn'd divers
Experiments and Notes about the *Producibleness of Chymical Principles.*

OXFORD,
Printed by *HENRY HALL* for *Ric. Davis,* and *B. Took* at the Ship in St. Pauls
Church-Yard. 1680.

Title page of Boyle's second edition of The Sceptical Chymist, *published in 1680.*

chemistry. It exposed flaws in the accepted theories about chemistry. It also provided insight into Boyle's ideas. Boyle's ideas were different from both the Aristotelian and the Paracelsian ideas. He thought the world was best understood in terms of matter and motion.[4] In his opinion, all substances were made of tiny, tiny particles. These particles, he believed, were all made of the same basic material. The particles could come together in many combinations that differed in "shape, size, motion or rest, and texture." These clusters of particles were called corpuscles.[5] Different corpuscles explained different substances.

Boyle's corpuscle chemistry was much less limiting than the other two theories. Aristotelians and Paracelsians always tried to explain substances in terms of very few factors. With Boyle's theory there could be many configurations of corpuscles. By doing experiments and carefully observing the results, one could learn more about the characteristics of substances and how they behaved.

In Boyle's time, more and more thinkers were

recognizing the value of basing scientific ideas on the evidence observed in experiments. Boyle was a leader in bringing this approach to chemistry. He argued for it in *The Sceptical Chymist*. He also practiced it in hundreds of chemical experiments.

Through experiments Boyle greatly expanded knowledge about the properties of many substances. Boyle was fascinated by colors. In his study of color, he discovered that he could use certain plant dyes to test whether substances were acids or alkalis. He used other chemical tests to identify substances, including copper and silver.[6] Boyle did extensive experiments with phosphorus, which he sometimes called icy noctiluca. White phosphorus glows at room temperature, a characteristic that intrigued Boyle.

The Sceptical Chymist played a role in the history of chemistry in three positive ways. First, it showed flaws in Aristotelian and Paracelsian chemistry. Second, it showed that chemistry could be thought of in terms of matter and motion using the corpuscle theory. Third, it

The ancient philosopher and scientist, Aristotle.

showed that experiments could reveal valuable information about the properties and behavior of substances.

The Sceptical Chymist is also famous for a paragraph included in the second edition of the book, published in 1680. Discussing the Aristotelian elements, Boyle wrote "I now mean by elements. . . certain primitive and simple, or perfectly unmingled bodies; which not being made of any other bodies, or of one another, are the ingredients, of which those called perfectly mixt bodies are immediately compounded, and into which they are ultimately resolved."[7]

This statement sounds very much like our modern definition of a chemical element. Today, a chemical element is often defined as "a substance that cannot be separated into different substances by ordinary chemical methods."[8]

Because of this similarity in words, many people have seized Boyle's statement as indicating that he discovered the modern element. As remarkable as Robert Boyle was, that was not among his accomplishments.

Boyle's questions and research were

About a hundred years after Boyle, French scientist Antoine Lavoisier (above) would make many important discoveries about chemical elements.

important steps in the long process that has led to our modern understanding of chemistry. About one hundred years after Boyle's definition, French chemist Antoine Lavoisier made important discoveries about chemical elements. From his experiments, Lavoisier considered elements to be substances that could not be broken down into other substances. He identified over thirty elements. The names Lavoisier gave many of them, including oxygen, are names we still use today.[9]

The Royal Society and the Gospel in New England

THE YEARS WHEN *THE SPRING OF THE AIR* and *The Sceptical Chymist* were published were a whirlwind for Robert Boyle. In the space of two years, he became one of the most famous scientific thinkers in England. At the same time, Boyle and his country were experiencing other changes.

England was finally entering a time of peace. King Charles I had been executed in 1649, but civil war and rebellions continued. In the 1650s Oliver Cromwell, a military leader, rose to power. After Cromwell died in 1658, his government crumbled under his son's rule.

Charles II, son of the executed King Charles I, had been living in exile. In 1660 he returned triumphantly to England. Tolerant and intelligent, King Charles II did not resume his father's battles.

When Charles II arrived in London, Robert Boyle was there to celebrate the king's return. While Boyle usually stayed out of politics, he was, like many in his family, in favor with the king.[1] Their father had supported Charles I. Within months of Charles II's return, he honored three of Boyle's brothers—Richard, Roger, and Francis—with titles. Richard, who was already Earl of Cork, also became Earl of Burlington. Roger was made Earl of Orrery. Francis became Viscount Shannon. The king offered Robert Boyle a title, too. Boyle declined it, apparently because he felt the responsibilities would take him from his interests.[2]

Just before the king's return, scholars interested in experimental science began meeting at Gresham College in London. As they became regular events, the meetings attracted thinkers from London and Oxford. King

Charles II was interested in science. He attended one evening and was entertained with a telescope "with which he viewed the heavens to his very great satisfaction."[3]

On November 28, 1660, the group heard Christopher Wren lecture about astronomy. After the lecture, Boyle and several others continued their discussion, in which "it was proposed that some course might be thought of to improve this meeting to a more regular way of debating things."[4] They decided to found an organization "for the promoting of experimental philosophy."[5]

Sir Robert Moray, a nobleman in the group, presented their idea of a scientific society to the king. A few days later he brought back news that Charles II was "well approved of it and would be ready to give an encouragement to it."[6] Over the next several months a charter was written. King Charles II signed the charter in 1662. The Royal Society was founded.

The Royal Society is an independent academy dedicated to promoting excellence in science. It is not a university or a government

The home of the Royal Society today. The organization occupies four townhouses in Carlton House Terrace in London.

agency. It is an organization most of whose members are scientists. The society provides support and funds to scientists to help them explore new frontiers of science. It publishes scientific books, papers, and journals. Many chemists, physicists, biologists, geologists, and other scientists around the world are members of today's Royal Society.

The Royal Society immediately started a library and collection of scientific instruments.

Boyle gave his first air pump to the organization. The society also began to publish scientific books. One of its first books was the splendid *Micrographia*, written and illustrated by Robert Hooke. In *Micrographia*, Hooke described and provided illustrations of observations he made with a microscope. It was the first major work that showed the microscopic world.

In 1662 Robert Hooke was appointed the Royal Society's first curator of experiments. Up to that time, he was Boyle's assistant. Hooke and Boyle continued to be close friends. They corresponded, did experiments together, and often shared dinner and conversation.

Robert Boyle was involved with the Royal Society from its founding almost to his death. He was asked to be the group's president, but declined the honor. At the society, Boyle did demonstrations of his experiments and reported on such diverse subjects as brazilwood, insects, vipers, and poisons.[7]

Boyle accepted few official appointments. However, in the early 1660s he entered into another long-term commitment with an

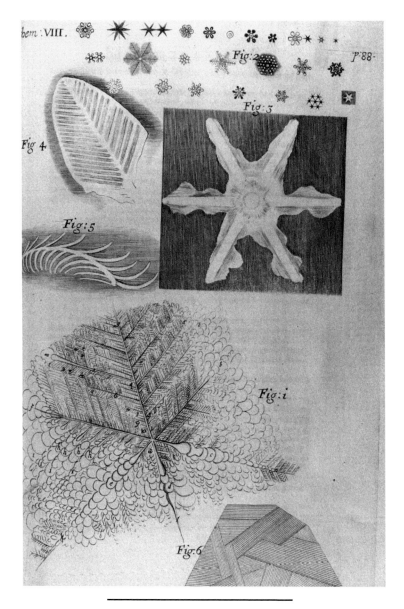

Robert Boyle's former assistant and long-time friend Robert Hooke was the Royal Society's first curator of experiments. Hooke used a microscope to examine insects, snowflakes, plants and other natural forms. Hooke's illustrations and descriptions of the things that he saw through the microscope were published in the book Micrographia. This snowflake, above, was among those images.

organization he supported. King Charles II appointed him governor of the Company for the Propagation of the Gospel in New England.

Boyle had a sincere desire to Christianize native populations outside of England.[8] One way he tried to achieve this was to translate and publish the Bible and other religious works into the languages of people he hoped to reach. While he was at Oxford, he paid Dr. Edward Pococke to translate a religious book into Arabic. Boyle paid for it to be published and distributed in Arab countries. He paid for the gospel to be translated into Malayan. He gave money to pay for religious translations into Turkish and contributed to publication of Welsh and Irish Bibles.

The purpose of the Company for the Propagation of the Gospel in New England was to convert Native Americans in New England to Christianity. As governor, Boyle served well. He was conscientious and "so genuinely concerned in the Company's affairs that he had every question referred to him for consideration."[9]

His position also put him in contact with many people in New England. They corresponded with him about company business. They also told him about interesting tidbits they had observed. Governor Winthrop in Connecticut wrote to him about a pond in which multitudes of fish suddenly died. Native Americans speculated that it might have been caused by lightning. Winthrop wanted to know if Boyle had ever heard of such an event.[10] William Penn, founder of Pennsylvania, wrote to Boyle about Native Americans, plants, and flowers. The Native Americans, he noted, "say little, but what they speak is fervent and elegant." "Of the flowers," Penn wrote, "I never saw larger, more variety, richer colors."[11]

For many years Boyle corresponded with and supported the missionary John Eliot. Eliot was a pastor in Massachusetts. He was dedicated to bringing Christianity to Native Americans. Eliot and his supporters established villages for "praying Indians," those who converted.[12] Natick, Massachusetts, was one of the fourteen communities they founded.

This engraving, published in the early 1800s, shows John Eliot preaching to the Indians. An ordained minister, he dedicated much of his life to bringing Christianity to American Indians. Eliot learned the local Algonquian language, wrote it down, and translated the Bible and prayer books.

To make Christianity accessible to Native Americans, Eliot learned their Algonquian language. He preached sermons in it. Eliot wrote down the native language by its sounds and translated the Bible into it. The company, and Boyle, supported many of Eliot's projects.

London

"I DID EXPECT AND HOPE THAT YOU would be in London before this. . . I being asked by everyone almost when you would be here," began a letter sent from Robert Hooke to Boyle in July 1663. Boyle still lived in Oxford, but he visited London frequently, especially for Royal Society meetings. Hooke regularly sent him detailed news of experiments. He reported on measuring vibrations of a pendulum,[1] observing the moons of Jupiter,[2] testing chemicals with a powder enclosed in iron,[3] and much more.

In Oxford, Boyle continued experimenting. He also published more books. Several of his books were scientific, examining his corpuscular theory and reporting his experiments. Others were about his philosophy and religion. *Some Considerations Touching the Usefulness of Experimental Natural Philosophy* expressed his view that science could help humankind to a better understanding of the world.[4] Boyle was religious. He believed that by understanding the world through science, people would have greater appreciation for God and God's design of the universe.

Experiments and Considerations Touching Colours was one of the scientific books Boyle wrote during this period. In *Colours*, he described fifty different experiments. Each one explored aspects of color. Some of the experiments dealt with "Whiteness and Blackness." For example, it was known that "a solution of silver" dyes hair black. Boyle carried that further and made a preparation of silver that appeared "snow-white," yet produced a "deep blackness, as if the stains had been made with ink."[5] In the book he showed how syrup made from violets changed color when exposed to different substances.

Boyle did not discover this color change himself, but he showed how it could be useful to chemists. He demonstrated that the syrup turned red when exposed to acids, such as vinegar or lemon juice. The syrup turned green when exposed to alkalis, such as ammonia. Being able to test substances was important to Boyle. Through tests he could be sure that he was using the same chemicals as he repeated experiments.

Boyle's visits to London were disrupted in 1665, when the bubonic plague struck the city. The plague was a deadly disease carried by fleas on rats. The plague was called the Black Death because black lumps on the skin were among its symptoms. Starting in the spring of 1665, a wave of death from the plague began. By summer it overwhelmed the city. In August alone, more than thirty thousand Londoners died of the plague. Wealthy people fled from the city. King Charles II and his court left London. The Royal Society adjourned. Boyle's friends Robert Hooke, William Petty, and Dr. Wilkins all left town together. They took scientific equipment with them so they could experiment elsewhere until it was safe to return.[6] With fall's cold weather, the plague slowed. Over 68,000 people in London died from the Black Death that year. King Charles II finally decided it was safe enough for him to return in February 1666.

Seven months later, disaster struck London again. Late at night on September 2, 1666, a fire broke out in a bakery on Pudding Lane. It was a windy night. Wooden houses with thatched roofs were crowded together along the narrow London streets. The flames spread quickly from Pudding Lane. The blaze tore through the neighborhood, then down to the docks by the river. Firefighters could not stop it. The fire burned out of control for three days. When it finally burned out, London was changed. It was estimated that thirteen thousand houses and eighty-nine churches were destroyed. Sixteen people were believed to have perished in the fire. Thousands and thousands more were left homeless.

Boyle's sister Katherine now lived in a mansion on an exclusive street named Pall Mall. Pall Mall was untouched by fire. Katherine went into "the poor city, which is thereby now turned indeed into a ruinous heap." She wrote to her brother, "I dispensed your charity amongst some poor families and persons that I found yet in the fields unhoused."[7]

London needed to be rebuilt. King Charles II appointed a commission to plan the reconstruction of the city. Boyle's friends Christopher Wren and Robert Hooke would play prominent roles. Wren designed fifty-five of the city's new churches. Hooke was appointed city surveyor and helped plan the new streets and arrangement of buildings.

Boyle was often in London during the year following the fire. He attended many Royal Society meetings. He arranged scientific demonstrations to entertain the Duchess of Newcastle and other visitors to the Society.

"I have ordered Thomas to look out for charcoal, and should gladly receive your order to put my back-house in posture to be employed by you," wrote Katherine to her brother in November 1667.[8] Katherine had invited Robert to move to her mansion. He could live there and have a laboratory for his experiments. Boyle accepted her invitation. Hooke advised Boyle on alterations to the house and helped set up his laboratory.

Robert Boyle was about forty-one years old when he moved to London. He had never married, although he was noted for his charm and his "agreeable conversation. . . among the ladies."[9] In London, a few of his friends urged him to consider marriage, and even suggested a bride. Boyle remained single.

Around the time that Boyle moved to London, Katherine's husband, Lord Ranelagh, died.[10] Once Robert was living in Pall Mall, the brother and sister entertained together. Hooke was a frequent guest in their home. Henry Oldenburg, secretary of the Royal Society, was a neighbor of Katherine's. He and his wife were often there, too.

Not only Londoners, but also visitors from abroad came to see Boyle. When the Grand Duke of Tuscany visited England, he "went in his carriage to the house of Mr. Robert Boyle, whose works have procured him the reputation of being one of the brightest geniuses in England."[11] Boyle showed him demonstrations with the air pump, experiments with colors, and a model of the moon.[12]

Poor health had almost always troubled Boyle. From the age of twenty, he believed he had a kidney stone. He attempted many cures for it but still suffered a great deal. He was prone to colds, fevers, and chills. Slender and frail, he regularly wore a cloak to stay warm. His eyes troubled him. Sometimes, he explained, it was as though he was seeing through a mist.[13]

In 1670 Boyle's health turned worse—he suffered a paralyzing stroke. He was so paralyzed that he could not "bring his hand to his mouth,"[14] but he was determined to recover. Every day he went outside for fresh air, even though he could not walk and had to be carried. He regularly had his feet and legs massaged and his arms and legs exercised. He also took a variety of medicines. A concoction made from "the dried flesh of vipers seemed to be one of the usefullest," he wrote.[15]

Boyle recovered to a considerable degree.

Robert Boyle's sister Katherine, Lady Ranelagh, lived on this London street called Pall Mall. Robert Boyle move into her home in 1668. Her house is no longer standing, but occupied half of the space now filled by the dark brick structure with light trim. The white house to the right was standing when Katherine and Boyle lived on Pall Mall.

Within a year of the stroke, he was back at the Royal Society, even putting on a demonstration for two noblemen who came from Italy.

Boyle did many experiments through the 1670s and 1680s. With his weak health and poor eyes, he employed assistants and servants to help him. They wrote down results and observations that he dictated to them. At his Pall Mall laboratory, Boyle had a new air pump. He continued his earlier work with air and developed new experiments, too. He was curious about the saltiness of seawater. By distilling it, he was able to separate out some salt. Of the distilled water he said, "we could not discern any saltiness by taste."[16]

In 1677 a gentleman from Germany named Johann Daniel Kraft visited Boyle. Kraft brought along a small quantity of a fascinating substance to show Boyle. To prepare the room for Kraft's demonstration, the shutters were closed and the candles were extinguished. In the dark, Kraft put a bit of the substance in a little glass sphere. The sphere began to glow. When Boyle shook it, it "appeared to shine more vividly."[17] Kraft scattered bits of the material on the carpet, where they twinkled like stars. He used the substance to write on a piece of paper. The letters glowed so brightly that they could be read on both sides of the paper.

The substance Kraft brought was phosphorus. Phosphorus is an element that occurs in many forms and in many places in nature. Phosphorus is in the human body and in plants and animals. It is found in certain rocks. White phosphorus is a form of phosphorus that glows at room temperature.

Boyle was intrigued by Kraft's display. During Kraft's first demonstration Boyle observed how phosphorus reacts with air. Kraft hinted to Boyle how phosphorus was obtained. A German alchemist who was trying to make gold had collected human urine. He allowed it to evaporate for several days and then distilled the remaining liquid. He did not produce gold, but one of the substances he did produce was phosphorus.

Boyle and his assistant, Ambrose Godfrey Hanckwitz, began trying to prepare their own phosphorus. Eventually, they were successful. Once he had a supply of the element, Boyle proceeded to do many experiments. He placed it in many different liquids—water, turpentine, clove oil, and more—to see how the phosphorus reacted. Using a magnifying glass to focus rays of sun on a fragment of phosphorus, he caused it to burst into flame. Through his experiments, Boyle was able to learn many of the characteristics of phosphorus. He wrote two books about it—*The Aerial Noctiluca* and *New Experiments and Observations Made with the Icy Noctiluca*. The substance was called both phosphorus and noctiluca in Boyle's time. Hanckwitz later went into business commercially preparing phosphorus. He was the leading producer of the element in Europe for forty years.

9
"Whose Writings They Most Desired"

"GLASSES, POTS, CHEMICAL AND mathematical instruments, books and bundles of papers, did so fill and crowd his bed-chamber, that there was but just room for a few chairs," wrote John Evelyn about Boyle's home at Pall Mall. "The mornings, after his private devotions, he usually spent in philosophic studies and in his laboratory," Evelyn explained. "In the afternoons he was seldom without company."[1]

Boyle lived with Katherine in London for more than twenty years. He kept up a busy pace of experimenting and writing. He had guests so frequently that from time to time he retreated to a private place elsewhere in London.[2] In 1689 his health worsened. Boyle wanted to settle his affairs and get his final writing done before he died. He resigned from his position as governor of the Company for the Propagation of the Gospel in New England. Although he was still a member of the Royal Society, he stopped his involvement in its day-to-day business.

Boyle published an advertisement, probably in 1689, "to those of his friends and acquaintances that are wont to do him the honour and favour of visiting him." He explained that his "skillful and friendly physician" and his "best friends" had advised him "against speaking daily with so many persons as are wont to visit him." He wrote in the advertisement that he wanted to get his papers "into some kind of order, that they may not remain useless." From then on he would only see guests on Tuesday and Friday mornings and Wednesday and Saturday afternoons.[3]

In his last years Boyle published more books.

One of them, *The Christian Virtuoso*, was about his conviction that science and religion are not in conflict with each other. Another was about observations of medicines, diamonds, and colors. A third, called *Medicina Hydrostatica*, was about determining specific gravity—the ratio of the density of a substance to the density of another substance. This was the first English book about this subject.[4]

In July 1691 Boyle wrote his last will and testament. As the year progressed, both he and his sister were failing. Katherine, Lady Ranelagh, died on December 23, 1691. Eight days later, Robert Boyle died early in the morning of December 31.

"England has lost her wisest man, wisdom her wisest son, and all Europe the man whose writings they most desired," wrote one friend of Boyle's on hearing of his death.[5] "He had the purity of an angel in him," wrote another.[6] A news article read, "The Honourable Mr. Boyle. . . hath ended his life with the year, to the unspeakable loss of the learned."[7]

A crowd "of persons of the best and noblest

quality, besides his own relations," attended Boyle's funeral.[8] He was buried at the St. Martin in the Fields Church. Apparently no memorial marked his grave. The old church was torn down in 1720 and replaced by the one that stands there today. However, no record exists of where the bodies were moved. Robert Boyle's grave site is now unknown.

In his will Boyle left gifts, money, and jewelry to family, friends, and servants. He also specified that certain of his papers be burned. (This instruction was not fully followed because many of those papers survived and were later published.) He left a generous sum of money to the Company for the Propagation of the Gospel in New England. His collections of minerals he bequeathed to the Royal Society. Boyle also arranged for a sum of money to be paid each year for lectures about the Christian religion. The first Boyle Lecture was held in February 1692. They have continued for over three hundred years.

Besides the money and gifts Boyle left in his will, he left a greater legacy to science. Robert

THE
General History
OF THE
AIR,

Designed and Begun

BY THE

Honble *ROBERT BOYLE* Esq.

IMPRIMATUR.
June 29. 1692.

Robert Southwell,
P. R. S.

LONDON,
Printed for *Awnsham* and *John Churchill,* at the Black
Swan in *Pater-noster-Row,* near *Amen-Corner.*
MDCXCII.

General History of Air *was one of Boyle's books that was published after his death.*

Boyle helped establish the scientific method in chemistry. He made discoveries about the properties of air. Through his questions and his experiments, Boyle showed the inadequacy of old ideas about substances. Boyle's life of science played a valuable role in the development of modern chemistry.

Activities

Activity One: Boyle's Law

Boyle's first scientific book, *New Experiments Physico-Mechanical Touching the Spring of the Air*, discussed many properties of air that he discovered using his air pump. One scholar, Franciscus Linus, criticized the book. Linus doubted that air could support weight as Boyle claimed. Boyle's response to Linus became known as Boyle's law. Boyle's law states that as the pressure upon a gas goes up, the volume of the gas goes down in the same proportion.

With this activity, you can see how air can be compressed. You will need:

- A florist's stem tube—this is a plastic tube and rubber lid with a hole in it. They are often used by florists to keep individual rose stems in water until they are put in a vase.

- A two-liter clear plastic soda bottle
- Water

Fill the clear plastic bottle with water. Push the stem tube into the filled bottle, with the rubber end down. Screw the top back on the bottle. Make sure it is tight. The tube will be bobbing near the top of the bottle.

Squeeze the bottle yourself, or get an adult to squeeze it for you. Squeezing the bottle puts pressure on it. Liquids, like water, do not compress. Gases, like air, do compress.

While still squeezing the bottle look at the stem tube inside it. Under the added pressure of your squeeze, water has squeezed into the stem tube. The air is still inside the tube, but it is occupying less space. The pressure on the bottle has compressed the air into a smaller space.

Now release the pressure on the bottle. With less pressure, the air expands and the water flows back out of the tube.

Activity Two: Air Pressure

On the surface of the earth, we live at the bottom of a sea of air. This sea is our atmosphere. In day-to-day life, air pressure is not only always pushing down on us but also in on all sides of us. (The exception to this is in special decompression rooms where pressure can be raised or lowered.) At sea level, the weight of air pressure is an average of 14.7 pounds per square inch.

In this experiment you can see how air pressure presses down on a common object. You will need

- A piece of balsa wood. You can usually buy it at a hardware store or craft store. A thin piece one inch wide and thirty inches long works well.
- A full sheet of newspaper

Fold the newspaper into sixteenths. (Start with the open sheet, fold it in half, fold it in half again, then twice more, alternating the fold along the length and width.) The folded paper will now be about 6 inches long and 5 inches across.

Lay your balsa-wood stick on a countertop so about half the stick is on the counter and about half is sticking out. Place the folded paper on the part of the stick that is on the counter. Give the other end of the stick that is off the counter a solid karate chop. What happened? The folded paper flew up in the air and the stick fell off the counter.

Now unfold the newspaper. Open it to full size and smooth it out. Again place the stick half on and half off the counter. Put the newspaper over the part of the stick that is on the counter. Give the stick a solid karate chop. What happened? The stick broke.

Why is it that the paper flew up in the first experiment but the stick broke in the second one? Both experiments used the same stick and the same piece of newspaper.

In the first experiment, air pressure was pressing down on a 5-inch by 6-inch surface— about 30 square inches. The force of your chop and the strength of the stick were enough to move the paper.

In the second experiment, air pressure was pressing down on a surface that was about 20 inches by 24 inches, or about 480 square inches. When you struck the stick, the stick was not strong enough to lift the paper under so much pressure. Each square inch of newspaper had 14.7 pounds of air pressing down on it, a total weight of over 7,000 pounds. The stick broke.

Activity Three: Invisible Ink

Robert Boyle did many experiments and made many observations about colors. He knew how to make invisible ink. One recipe that he wrote for invisible ink required vinegar and lead. When his ink was wiped with a solution made with lime, the invisible message was revealed.

Here is an easy recipe for invisible ink. You need:

- A lemon
- Paper
- Electric iron
- Small paintbrush or cotton swab

Cut the lemon in half and squeeze it, collecting its juice in a bowl. Dip your paintbrush or cotton swab in the lemon juice. Write your message on the paper. Let the paper dry. With adult assistance turn an electric iron to a high setting. Use the hot iron to press your paper. In a short time your hidden message will appear, in a light brown color.

Why did the letters appear? Lemon juice contains citric acid. Where the acid was applied to the paper, the paper was weakened. Under the hot iron the weakened paper began to burn before the stronger paper.

Chronology

1627—January 25: Robert Boyle is born at Lismore Castle, Ireland.

1635—Goes to Eton College in England with his brother Francis. Studies at Eton for about two years.

1639—Leaves England with Isaac Marcombes to travel and study on the continent.

1640—During a violent thunderstorm in Geneva, Boyle resolves to lead his life more religiously.

1643—Father dies.

1644—Returns to England. England in midst of civil war.

1646—Moves to Stalbridge. Letters indicate that he is interested in experiments.

1649—The furnace Boyle needs for chemical experiments arrives. His enthusiasm for experimenting grows.

1656—Boyle moves to Oxford.

1660—Publishes *New Experiments Physico-Mechanical Touching the Spring of the Air*.

This work presents many of Boyle's experiments with the air pump. King Charles II returns to England. Boyle and other scientific thinkers found the Royal Society. (Its official charter is granted in 1662.)

1661—Publishes *The Sceptical Chymist*, his book refuting the accepted Aristotelian and Paracelsian views of chemistry. During this same year he conducts further experiments with air, including one that reveals Boyle's law.

Appointed governor of the Company for the Propagation of the Gospel in New England.

1662—Publishes second edition of *Spring of the Air*. This edition includes the experiments that demonstrate Boyle's law.

1664—Writes *Experiments and Considerations Touching Colours*.

1665—Bubonic plague strikes London. More than 68,000 die.

1666—Great fire of London. More than three-quarters of the inner city of London burned.

1668—Moves to his sister's home in London.

1670—Suffers paralyzing stroke, but within a year recovers to a considerable degree.

1671—Almost every year from 1671 to his death, Boyle publishes at least one book or essay about science, religion, or his view of the relationship between the two subjects.

1680—Publishes second edition of *The Sceptical Chymist*.

1680–1681—Publishes two books about his experiments with phosphorus.

1689—In failing health, he needs to limit time to see visitors.

1691—Dies early in the morning of December 31.

Chapter Notes

Chapter 1. "Which Seems to Prove..."

1. Robert Boyle, *The Works of Robert Boyle*, eds. Michael Hunter and Edward B. Davis (London: Pickering & Chatto, 1999), vol. I, p. 230.

2. Ibid.

3. Ibid.

Chapter 2. One Who Loves Virtue

1. Louis Trenchard More, *The Life and Works of the Honourable Robert Boyle* (New York: Oxford University Press, 1944), p. 18.

2. Ibid., p. 5.

3. Ibid., p. 13.

4. Robert Boyle, *The Works*, 3rd ed., ed. Thomas Birch (Hildesheim: Georg Olms Verlagsbuchhandlung, 1965), vol. I, p. xiii.

5. Ibid.

6. Ibid.

7. Ibid.

8. Ibid.

9. Ibid.

10. Ibid.

11. R.E.W. Maddison, *The Life of the Honourable Robert Boyle, F.R.S.* (London: Taylor and Francis, 1969), p.185.

12. Boyle, vol. I, p. xiv.

13. Ibid.

14. Maddison, p. 11, footnote.

15. Boyle, vol. I, p. xvii.

16. Ibid., vol. I, p. xviii.

17. Ibid., p. xxii.

18. Ibid.

19. Ibid.

20. Ibid. vol. I, p. xxiv.

21. More, p. 50.

Chapter 3. "Transported and Bewitched"

1. R.E.W. Maddison, *The Life of the Honourable Robert Boyle, F.R.S.* (London: Taylor and Francis, 1969), p. 53.

2. Louis Trenchard More, *The Life and Works of the Honourable Robert Boyle* (New York: Oxford University Press, 1944), p. 54.

3. Ibid.

4. Ed Klekowski, "Charles I, Parliament, and the English Civil War," n.d., <www.bio.umass.edu/biology/conn.river/regicide.html> (March 1, 2004).

5. More, p. 58.

6. Maddison, p. 70.

7. Ibid.

8. Ibid., p. 71.

9. Robert Boyle, *The Works*, 3rd ed., ed. Thomas Birch (Hildesheim: Georg Olms Verlagsbuchhandlung, 1965), vol. VI, pp. 49–50.

10. Maddison, p. 76.

11. More, p. 214.

12. Ibid., p. 76.

13. Boyle, vol. VI, p. 634.

14. More, p. 87.

15. Ibid., p. 79.

16. Ibid., p. 92.

17. Maddison, p. 89.

18. More, p. 90.

19. Ibid., p. 86.

20. Ibid., p. 92.

Chapter 4. *The Spring of the Air*

1. Richard Westfall, "Hooke, Robert," *Dictionary of Scientific Biography*, ed. Charles Coulston Gillispie (New York: Scribners, 1973), vol. 6, p. 487.

2. Mario Gliozzi, "Torricelli, Evangelista," *Dictionary of Scientific Biography*, ed. Charles Coulston Gillispie (New York: Scribners, 1973), vol. 13, p. 438.

3. Louis Trenchard More, *The Life and Works of the Honourable Robert Boyle* (New York: Oxford University Press, 1944), p. 94.

4. Robert Boyle, *The Works*, 3rd ed., ed. Thomas Birch (Hildesheim: Georg Olms Verlagsbuchhandlung, 1965), vol. I, p. 7.

5. Robert Boyle, *The Works of Robert Boyle*, eds. Michael Hunter and Edward B. Davis (London: Pickering & Chatto, 1999), vol. I, p. 174.

6. Ibid.

7. Ibid.

8. Ibid.

9. Mario Gliozzi, "Torricelli, Evangelista," *Dictionary of Scientific Biography*, ed. Charles Coulston Gillispie (New York: Scribners, 1973), vol. 13, p. 438.

10. J. J. O'Connor and E. F. Robertson, "Evangelista Torricelli," November 2002, <www-gap.dcs.st-and.ac.uk/history/Mathematicians/Torricelli.html> (March 1, 2004).

11. Ibid.

12. Ibid.

13. More, p. 94.

Chapter 5. Boyle's Law

1. Robert Boyle, *The Works*, 3rd ed., ed. Thomas Birch (Hildesheim: Georg Olms Verlagsbuchhandlung, 1965), vol. II, p. 287.

2. Ibid., vol. I, p. lxiii.

3. R.E.W. Maddison, *The Life of the Honourable Robert Boyle, F.R.S.* (London: Taylor and Francis, 1969), p. 225.

4. Boyle, vol. I, p. 158.

5. Ibid.

6. Ibid., vol. I, p. 159.

7. Robert E. Krebs, *The History and Use of Our Earth's Chemical Elements, 3rd College Edition* (New York: Simon & Schuster, Inc., 1988), p. 9.

Chapter 6. *The Sceptical Chymist*

1. Lawrence M. Principe, *The Aspiring Adept: Robert Boyle and His Alchemical Quest* (Princeton: Princeton University Press, 1998), pp. 28–29.

2. Ibid.

3. Robert Boyle, *The Works*, 3rd ed., ed. Thomas Birch (Hildesheim: Georg Olms Verlagsbuchhandlung, 1965), vol. I, p. 570.

4. Marie Boas Hall, "Robert Boyle," *Dictionary of Scientific Biography*, ed. Charles Coulton Gillispie (New York: Scribners, 1973), vol. 2, p. 378.

5. R.E.W. Maddison, *The Life of the Honourable Robert Boyle, F.R.S.* (London: Taylor and Francis, 1969), p. 104.

6. Hall, vol. 2, p. 381.

7. Boyle, vol. I, p. 562.

8. Webster's New World Dictionary and Thesaurus.

9. Robert E. Krebs, *The History and Use of Our Earth's Chemical Elements, 3rd College Edition* (New York: Simon & Schuster, Inc., 1988), p. 10.

Chapter 7. The Royal Society and the Gospel in New England

1. R.E.W. Maddison, *The Life of the Honourable Robert Boyle, F.R.S.* (London: Taylor and Francis, 1969), p. 112.

2. Louis Trenchard More, *The Life and Works of the Honourable Robert Boyle* (New York: Oxford University Press, 1944), pp. 105–106.

3. Maddison, p. 99.

4. Ibid., pp. 99–100.

5. Ibid.

6. Ibid., p. 100.

7. Ibid., p. 102.

8. More, p. 117.

9. Maddison, p. 102.

10. Robert Boyle, *The Works*, 3rd ed., ed. Thomas Birch (Hildesheim: Georg Olms Verlagsbuchhandlung, 1965), vol. VI, p. 582.

11. Ibid., vol. VI, p. 659.

12. Ibid.

Chapter 8. London

1. Robert Boyle, *The Works*, 3rd ed., ed. Thomas Birch (Hildesheim: Georg Olms Verlagsbuchhandlung, 1965), vol. VI, p. 490.

2. Ibid., vol. VI, p. 495.

3. Ibid., vol. VI, p. 494.

4. Ibid., vol. I, p. XV.

5. Ibid., vol. I, p. 714.

6. Louis Trenchard More, *The Life and Works of the Honourable Robert Boyle* (New York: Oxford University Press, 1944), p. 124.

7. R.E.W. Maddison, *The Life of the Honourable Robert Boyle, F.R.S.* (London: Taylor and Francis, 1969), p. 127.

8. More, p. 127.

9. Ibid., p. 134.

10. Ibid., p. 128.

11. Maddison, p. 143.

12. Ibid., p. 144.

13. Ibid., p. 181.

14. More, p. 130.

15. Ibid., p. 131.

16. Boyle, vol. III, p. 771.

17. Maddison, p. 159.

Chapter 9. "Whose Writings They Most Desired"

1. R.E.W. Maddison, *The Life of the Honourable Robert Boyle, F.R.S.* (London: Taylor and Francis, 1969), p. 187.

2. Ibid.

3. Ibid., p. 177.

4. Ibid., p. 178.

5. Ibid., p. 188.

6. Ibid., p. 185.

7. Ibid., p. 191.

8. Ibid., p. 185.

Glossary

acids—In chemistry, substances that are compounds of hydrogen, when they react with a base, or alkali, produce a salt. Acetic acid is in vinegar; citric acid is in lemons.

air—Colorless, odorless mixture of gases that envelope the earth and is breathed by mammals. Air is a combination of gases including oxygen, nitrogen, and carbon dioxide.

air pressure—The pressure of atmospheric air.

alchemy—The chemistry of the Middle Ages, a pseudoscience whose practitioners attempted to transmute substances into gold.

alkalis—Substances also called bases. Their characteristics include the ability to neutralize acids, producing a salt. Baking soda, potash, and ammonia are common alkalis.

anatomy—Dissecting a plant or animal in order to understand its parts or structure.

chemistry—The branch of physical science that deals with substances, or forms of matter, the laws that govern them, their characteristics, and how they behave when exposed to different substances and conditions.

corpuscle—A tiny body or particle of matter.

dissect—To cut a plant or animal into pieces to learn about its structure or parts.

distill—To vaporize and condense a substance by heating and cooling it.

element—One of the simple substances of which all matter is composed.

kidney stone—A hard mineral deposit that sometimes forms in the kidney.

molecule—The smallest portion a substance can be divided into and still retain its characteristics.

Parliament—The legislative branch of the government of Great Britain and certain other countries.

piston—A disk that fits snugly inside a cylinder and can be moved back and forth.

pressure—The force exerted on one body by another through its weight.

pump—A mechanical device, often using a piston and cylinder, used to raise or move a liquid, such as water, or a gas, such as air.

rhetoric—The art of using language to influence others.

stammer—To falter or stumble in speech, sometimes repeating sounds or syllables.

stutter—To speak with an involuntary repetition of sounds or syllables.

transmute—To change one substance into another.

treason—Betrayal of one's country.

vacuum—A space entirely empty of matter.

volume—A quantity or amount. The space occupied in three dimensions.

Further Reading

Hunter, Michael, ed. *Robert Boyle Reconsidered*. New York: Cambridge University Press, 1994.

Kuslan, L. & A. Stone. *Robert Boyle: The Great Experimenter*. Upper Saddle River, N.J.: Prentice Hall, 1994.

Tiner, John Hudson. *Robert Boyle: Trailblazer of Science*. Fenton, Mich.: Mott Media, 1989.

Tiner, John Hudson. *100 Scientists Who Shaped World History*. San Mateo, Calif.: Bluewood Books, 2000.

Internet Addresses

The Robert Boyle Project, University of London

http://www.bbk.ac.uk/Boyle/

Robert Boyle: Mighty Chemist

http://www.woodrow.org/teachers/chemistry/
institutes/1992/Boyle.html

Robert Boyle and Robert Hooke, University College, Oxford

http://web.comlab.ox.ac.uk/oxinfo/univ-col/
boyle-hooke.html

Index